After School Stuff
Cool Crafts

written by Cara J. Stevens
Illustrated by Chris Sabatino

LOWELL HOUSE JUVENILE

LOS ANGELES

NTC/Contemporary Publishing Group

Published by Lowell House
A division of NTC/Contemporary Publishing Group, Inc.
4255 West Touhy Avenue, Lincolnwood (Chicago), Illinois 60646-1975 U.S.A.

Managing Director and Publisher: Jack Artenstein
Director of Publishing Services: Rena Copperman
Editorial Director: Brenda Pope-Ostrow
Project Editor: Amy Downing
Designer: Treesha R. Vaux

Library of Congress Catalog Card Number: 97-73112

ISBN 0-7373-0241-0

Lowell House books can be purchased at special discounts when ordered in bulk for
premiums and special sales. Contact Customer Service at the address above, or call 1-800-323-4900.

Printed and bound in the United States of America

DHD 10 9 8 7 6 5 4 3 2 1

Contents

Desk Decoupage

Does it seem like grown-ups are always telling you to keep things tidy? Keep your pencils, papers, and other stuff organized with a desk set you made yourself!

What you'll need:

- newspapers
- smock or old shirt
- spoon
- 1 cup clear-drying glue
- ½ cup water
- small disposable aluminum pie pan
- ruler
- 4 empty matchboxes
- clean, empty can (a soup or vegetable can works best)
- cardboard box lid, at least 8½ x 11
- paper towels
- scissors
- wrapping paper, comics, or old magazines
- wet towel
- craft paintbrush
- lacquer or shellac (optional)
- 4 Y-fasteners (round head paper fasteners)

What to do:

1 Spread some of the newspapers over your work area and on the floor, and put on a smock or old shirt so you don't ruin your favorite clothes.

2 With a spoon, mix together the glue and water in a small pie pan, and set it aside.

3 Rip the remaining newspapers into lots of strips about 3 inches wide. You will be covering your desk set in newspaper first. The matchboxes will turn into a small set of drawers, the can will become a pencil cup, and the cardboard box lid will be a tray to hold your blank loose-leaf paper or your completed homework assignments.

4 Dip a newspaper strip into the glue mixture, coating both sides. Smooth it over the top of the cardboard box lid. Keep dipping the strips into the glue and layering them on top of each other until the lid is covered. Wipe off any excess drippy glue with a paper towel. Cover the can with newsprint as well, crisscrossing the strips and keeping each layer as smooth as possible. Leave the bottom of each desk-set piece uncovered. Glue the four small boxes together two across and two down so that they form a chest of drawers. Cover with newspaper. Be sure the drawers open and close.

5 While your desk set is drying, cut out shapes, comics, or designs from wrapping paper or magazines to decorate the set of drawers, the pencil cup, and the tray.

6 Dip each cutout into the glue mixture, thickly coating each piece. Press each cutout on the set of drawers, tray, and pencil cup in a pattern or just randomly. Wipe your hands on the wet towel when they start feeling too goopy. Continue gluing the cutouts on the surface until each item is completely covered. Keep the bottom plain to make working and drying easier.

7 When your desk-set pieces are covered, dip the paintbrush in the glue mixture and paint over the entire area of each item to smooth out any wrinkles, then let them dry. To give your set an old-fashioned look, paint over everything with a coat of lacquer or shellac after the glue has dried.

8 Find the center of the front of each matchbox drawer, then poke the Y-fastener through the front of each drawer to form a handle. Spread the two ends of each Y-fastener inside the drawer so that it stays put.

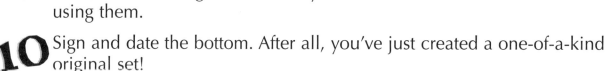

9 Let all three pieces dry completely (at least an hour) before setting them out on your desk and using them.

10 Sign and date the bottom. After all, you've just created a one-of-a-kind original set!

Now that you have a handy-dandy desk set, you may as well actually study!
A few tips:

1. Don't have music or the TV on.
2. When you sit down to work, allow yourself at least a 10-minute break every hour, especially if you're working at a computer.
3. If you're faced with a lot of work, set small goals for yourself by writing them down and checking them off as you complete them.
4. For long-term projects, do a little bit each day so you're not faced with an overwhelming task the night before a project is due.

What has an e at the beginning and an e at the end and only contains one letter? **An envelope.**

Friendship Key Chain

These colorful key chains are so easy to make, you can give one to each of your pals!

What you'll need:

➡ five 24-inch pieces of embroidery string in different colors
⇨ tape
➡ ruler
⇨ key ring

What to do:

1 Hold the five pieces of string so that the ends match up. Tie them all together in a simple knot at the top. Tape the knot to the end of a table, and move back from the table with all five strings in your hand.

2 Twist the strands together in one direction until it is about 17 inches long, then tie a knot in the end. Hold the end of the strands in one hand, and place a finger of your other hand in the center of the twist. Fold the end up toward the knot at the top.

3 When you remove your finger from the loop, the strings will twist around themselves automatically. You may need to smooth them out a bit by pulling very gently on the loop.

4 Remove the tape while holding the ends of the strings. Tie the ends together in a simple knot. Slip the looped end of the key chain into the key ring the same way you would put on a key.

5 Now that you know how easy they are to make, create key chains for all your friends!

Downhill Rollers

These small cars really go, as long as they're heading downhill. Make the two models below, set up a downhill course, and see which one goes faster.

What you'll need:

➡ chunk of polymer or modeling clay (about 2 fistfuls)

⇨ ruler

➡ plastic knife

⇨ 4 toothpicks

➡ craft glue

⇨ playing-card box or the inside of a large empty matchbox

What to do:

1. Rip off half of the clay and mold it into any car shape. Roll the rest of the clay into one short cylinder about 3 inches long and 1 inch wide. Cut the cylinder in half and put half aside.

2. To make the wheels, cut one cylinder into four equal discs. Poke two toothpicks through the bottom of the clay car to form axles for the wheels. Twist them back and forth to widen the holes enough for the wheels to spin freely.

3. Dab a little glue on the end of each toothpick and insert a wheel onto each toothpick end. Set this car aside.

4. Poke both remaining toothpicks all the way through your card box or matchbox to create the wheel axles. Twist them to enlarge the holes so they can move freely.

MATCHES

5 Cut the remaining clay cylinder into four equal discs, or wheels. Dab glue on the end of the toothpicks and insert a wheel onto each toothpick end.

6 Test each car to make sure it rolls properly. You may need to widen the toothpick holes to make the wheels move more easily.

7 Set up a downhill course on a sidewalk, plank, or paved hill and let 'em roll! When you see how they move, you can adjust the cars to make them move more efficiently.

To set up a mini racecourse, you'll need to start the cars at the top of a hill to give them momentum. Prop up one end of a thin piece of cardboard on a stack of books or blocks, and clear a path at the foot of the hill. Test each car to see which one rolls farther and which goes faster.

CYCLIPS

What do you call a one-eyed monster that holds paper? A Cyclips!

What you'll need:

➡ paper towels

⇨ 2 x 9-inch piece of green felt

➡ ruler

⇨ large clothespin (either wooden or plastic) with wire hinge

➡ white glue

⇨ cotton ball

➡ ½ x 3-inch piece of red felt

⇨ googly eye

What to do:

1 Line your work space with paper towels.

2 Fold the green felt in half so that it is now 2 x 4½ inches. Hold the clothespin open as far as you can without breaking it. Dab glue along the inside of the clothespin, then lay the folded felt inside the clothespin with the fold butted up against the hinge of the clothespin. This is the inside of the Cyclips's mouth. Close the clothespin with the felt hanging out.

3 Dab glue along the top of the clothespin. Place the cotton ball on top of the clothespin, 1 inch back from the open edge of the clip. This will be the bulge for its forehead. Dab glue over the top of the cotton ball, then lay the top flap of green felt along the top of the clothespin and the cotton ball.

4 Dab glue along the bottom of the clothespin and attach the bottom flap to it.

5 Hold the clothespin open and dab glue along the bottom of the inside of the Cyclips's mouth. Place the red felt along the glue to form a long tongue hanging out of the mouth.

6 Dab glue on the googly eye and place it in the center of the monster's forehead. Wipe off any excess glue, and set it aside to dry.

7 When your Cyclips is dry, you can use it to hold papers, clip your lunch bag closed, hold your keys, or just keep you company clipped onto your backpack.

You might want to give your Cyclips a name—after all, even monsters have feelings!

GRAFFITI LUNCH BAG

If you bring your lunch to school in a disposable bag every day for a year, you'll have thrown out over 200 paper bags. That's a lot of trees—and a lot of garbage. Why not bring your lunch in a sack that has personality and saves trees at the same time? You can change the design as often as you want so it will seem like you have a new lunch bag every week!

What you'll need:

➡ water-based markers
⇨ plain canvas lunch bag

What to do:

1 Using the washable markers on your lunch bag, draw the logo of your favorite band, your school mascot, or anything else that comes to mind. You can ask friends to draw on your lunch bag, too.

2 Throw the lunch bag into the wash at the end of each week, and every week you can have a fresh canvas for a new theme.

The best way to recycle is to reuse things. Take an old box and fill it with old stuff such as bottles, cans, paper-towel rolls, and junk mail. Label it "Craft Stuff" and use it when you want to make Cool Crafts!

THE GREAT, GROWING SPONGE

Grow an indoor garden of flowers, fruits, or vegetables!

What you'll need:

➡ scissors

➡ sponges

➡ plates or shallow bowls

➡ quick-sprouting seed packets (try marigold, pumpkin, grass, mustard, parsley, lima bean, sweet pea, or viola seeds)

➡ tray

➡ cheesecloth

➡ spray bottle of water

What to do:

1 Using scissors, cut the sponges into different shapes, such as ducks, dogs, or people's heads.

2 Wet each sponge, then wring it out so it's damp but not completely wet. Place each sponge on a plate or in a shallow bowl. Sprinkle each sponge with a different kind of seed, then place all the plates and bowls onto the tray. Cover the tray with the cheesecloth and spray it with some water to moisten it.

3 Place the tray in a sunny spot but not in direct sunlight. Take off the cheesecloth during the day and keep the sponges moist with the spray bottle. At night, cover the tray with the cheesecloth and moisten it again with the spray bottle.

4 It takes about a half hour to create this project and only a few minutes to check on it each day. In a few days, you will start seeing results!

Brown-Bag Book Covers

Keep your books under wraps with book covers that double as great reading material.

What you'll need:

➡ scissors

⇨ large plain paper bag

➡ book to be covered

⇨ ruler

➡ comics or trading cards

⇨ glue, tape, or rubber cement

➡ clear, self-adhesive paper (optional)

What to do:

1 Cut along one of the side seams of the paper bag, then cut out the bottom so you are left with a long, flat sheet. If there is writing on the bag, it should lie faceup.

2 Set the book on the paper, front-side up and about 5 inches away from the right side of the sheet (or half the width of the book cover).

3 Fold the left side of the sheet up and over the book so it looks like you're wrapping it up completely. Stretch the left side out so it is even with the right edge, about 5 inches beyond the edge of the book. Trim off the excess paper. At the top and bottom of the book, fold the paper down to align with the top and bottom edges. Lift the book, and tuck the extra paper behind the book. Set the book back in its place.

Why was the math book sad? *Because it had too **many** problems.*

4 Open the front cover of the book and slide the cover into the slot made by the folds. Do the same with the back cover.

5 Decorate your book cover with comics, baseball cards, or other trading cards using glue, tape, or rubber cement.

6 To make it last extra long, cover the front, back, and sides with a layer of clear, self-adhesive paper.

TOP 10 STUDY SNACKS
1. Frozen banana on a Popsicle® stick
2. Trail mix
3. Peanut butter and jelly on crackers
4. Apple or celery with peanut butter
5. Granola bars
6. Fruit smoothies
7. Low-fat yogurt
8. Cheese and crackers
9. Hard-boiled eggs
10. Chips and salsa

Dancing Clown

Pull the string and watch the clown dance. This happy clown is great for keeping you company while you study.

What you'll need:

→ pencil

⇨ sheet of thin cardboard (the top or bottom of a white gift box works)

→ scissors

⇨ 4 Y-fasteners (round head paper fasteners)

→ colored markers

⇨ craft glue

→ small scraps of fabric

⇨ tiny pom-pom

→ yarn

⇨ string

→ 4 or more tiny bells

⇨ bead

→ nail or peg (optional)

What to do:

1 Using the pencil, create the outline of your clown on the cardboard by drawing the body, head, and hat as one piece and each arm and leg separately. Cut the pieces out with your scissors.

What do you call a scared tyrannosaurus? **A nervous rex.**

2 Place the arms and legs behind the body, and hold them in place with Y-fasteners by sticking each fastener first through the body, then an arm or leg, and then spreading the edges of the fastener outward to hold it in place.

3 Using your colored markers, draw features on your clown such as a happy face, a hat, and other details. Glue on the scraps of fabric for clothing.

4 Glue the pom-pom to the top of the clown's hat. You can also use a pom-pom for the nose. Glue on the yarn for hair. Color in the remaining features with your markers.

5 Cut four small lengths of string. Thread each string through a small bell, then wrap one string around each of the clown's wrists and ankles and tie it in a knot at the back. Hold the strings in place with a dab of glue on the back of the wrists and ankles. Cut another small piece of string, tie it in a loop, and glue it to the top of the clown's head to use as a hanger.

6 Turn the clown over so that its back is facing you. Cut two pieces of string. Tie one piece to one arm fastener and stretch it across to the other arm fastener and tie it in a knot. Tie the other piece of string to the two leg fasteners on the clown's back.

7 Cut a long piece of string and tie one end to the middle of the arm string. Drop the other end down and knot it once around the center of the leg string. Let the string hang down several inches below the clown and tie a bead to the end of the string as a pull handle.

8 Hang the loop on a nail or peg. Pull the bead and watch your clown dance and listen as its arms and legs fly up and jingle!

Make a whole dancing circus with a weight lifter, a dancing bear, a tightrope walker holding an umbrella, and anything else you can think of.

Guatemalan Worry Dolls

In some parts of Central America, children tell one worry to each doll and place the dolls under their pillow when they go to bed at night. In the morning, because they believe in the dolls, the children wake up to discover the dolls have taken their worries away. You may want to try this yourself the night before a big test!

What you'll need:

➡ 1 sheet of 8½ x 11-inch loose-leaf paper (enough for 2 worry dolls)

➡ scissors

➡ ruler

➡ pen or pencil

➡ embroidery floss or yarn in 3 or more colors (1 color for the head, 1 for the body and arms, and 1 for the legs)

➡ glue stick or craft glue

➡ clear tape

➡ cotton ball

What to do:

1 Fold the paper in half lengthwise, then cut along the center fold so you have two long, thin strips. Set one strip aside.

2 Using the ruler, mark off 6 inches on the piece of paper, then fold the paper along that line. Cut along the fold. Your paper should now be 6 inches long by 4¼ inches wide. Save the remaining paper for the arms.

3 Roll the rectangle of paper lengthwise into a tight roll 6 inches long. Fold the roll in half. The top of

¾

1½

the fold will be the head for your doll. The two ends will form the legs. Make a waist mark halfway down the roll to separate the legs from the body. Mark off ¾ inch from the top of the paper to form the head.

4. Take a piece of embroidery floss and glue it to the paper at the center mark. Wind the floss tightly up the body. Stop winding at the mark for the head. Wind the floss back down to the doll's waist, then back up again until that area is completely covered. Glue down the end of the floss, and use tape to hold it until the glue dries.

5. Cut the floss you want to use for the head, and glue one end to the top of the head. Wrap the head until no white paper shows. Glue down the other end, holding it with tape until the glue dries. For the hair, cut and style a piece of a cotton ball into your favorite hairstyle and glue it to the top of the head.

6. To wrap the legs, start at one foot and glue down the end of the thread, then wind it tightly up one leg and down the other and back so that no white paper shows. Glue down the end and secure it with tape until the glue has dried.

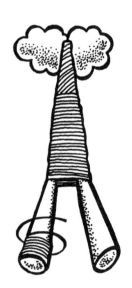

7. For the arms, take the piece of paper you set aside in step 2, cut it in half, and set one piece aside. Roll it into a tight roll, fold it in half, then unfold it so there is a seam in the middle where it will attach to the body. Wrap the roll in the same color floss as the body. Then glue the center of the roll to the body just below the head. Wind the thread over and around the body at least 10 times to hold the arms in place, then cut and glue the end in place, holding it with tape.

8 Once the glue has dried, remove the tape in all spots. Make a second doll with the rest of the paper. You may also want to create a whole set of worry dolls with different-colored "costumes" and keep them by your bedside to tell them your troubles at night!

Worry dolls make great accessories and gifts. Attach a small doll to the top of a package, a barrette, a hair clip, or a safety pin.

Pencil Pal

Do you get lonely when you're doing your homework? This Pencil Pal doesn't just keep you company, it also helps you do your work. It can double as an eraser (though it may tend to get a bit bent out of shape!).

What you'll need:

→ newspapers

⇨ smock or old shirt

→ scissors

⇨ kneadable eraser

→ 2 pencils

⇨ acrylic paint and paintbrush (optional)

→ glitter, paper clips, seed beads, glitter, or pipe cleaners

What to do:

1 Spread newspapers on the table and on the floor around your work area, and put on a smock or old shirt.

2 Cut the kneadable eraser in half. Wrap one half around the end of a pencil, and pinch together the sides and top. Use your fingertips to mold and smooth the eraser into a long, thin blob.

3 Pull a small piece from the unused half of the eraser. Shape it into a nose and press it on the eraser on the pencil to form a face. Make more shapes to add big eyes, long ears, bushy eyebrows, horns, or a handlebar mustache. Using your fingers, sculpt cheeks and a chin. Carve a big grin using the sharpened tip of the other pencil.

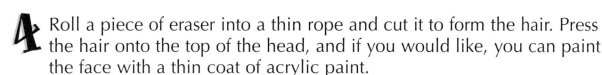

4. Roll a piece of eraser into a thin rope and cut it to form the hair. Press the hair onto the top of the head, and if you would like, you can paint the face with a thin coat of acrylic paint.

5. Add on the finishing touches with decorative glitter, paper-clip eyeglasses, seed-bead earrings or hair clips, or pipe-cleaner antennae.

To liven up your pencil case, create a whole Pencil Pal family!

Box Your Memories

If you're suffering from those back-to-school blues, preserve your summer or winter vacation in a box and take a trip using your imagination any time you want.

What you'll need:

➡ scissors

➡ road maps from your trip

➡ white or clear glue

➡ shoe box or small cardboard box with a lid

➡ dark marker

➡ white paper

➡ notebook small enough to fit inside box

➡ pencil or pen

➡ photos from trip

➡ postcards from trip

➡ found objects from trip

What to do:

1 Cut the map into pieces. Glue the strips onto the box, either straight across or in random patches. Cover the box and lid completely with the map.

2 Using a dark marker, write the name of the place you went and the date of your trip on a strip of white paper. Glue the paper onto the top or side of the box.

3 On the first page or the cover of the notebook, write where you went and who you went with. Use the rest of the notebook to write down what you did each day in as much detail as you can remember. Months or years from now, you will be happy you did.

4 On the back of each photo, write where and when each one was taken and the names of the people in the picture. You can even write a little story to give some background to the photo. Gather together some postcards of special places you saw. On the back of each card, jot a note on its significance. Also include any small objects you collected on your trip. Write a description of each item in your notebook, along with where you found it. Put all the items inside the box with the notebook.

Memorabilia is stuff you collect to remind you of something, such as a seashell to remind you of a trip to the beach, a ticket stub to remind you of a concert, or a flower to remind you of the person who gave it to you. You can make a memorabilia box for anything, such as this year's Little League season, your first dance recital, or a weekend trip to Grandma's house.

Radical Rain Stick

More than half of the world's plant and animal species inhabit the 7 percent of the world that is covered in rain forest. Many of these species are located in small parts of the rain-forest ecosystems and are found nowhere else on Earth. There are rain forests all over the world, from Costa Rica to Alaska. This rain stick mimics the sound made by rain in the rain forests.

What you'll need:

➡ pushpin

➡ long wrapping-paper tube, 1½ inches wide

➡ toothpicks

➡ masking tape

➡ electrical tape

➡ funnel

➡ uncooked rice, gravel, beads, unpopped popcorn, or sand (each one makes a different kind of sound)

➡ colored contact paper (optional)

What to do:

1 Poke the pushpin into the tube about 40 to 50 times, up and down the tube and on all sides.

2 Push a toothpick into each hole and break off the ends carefully so that the toothpick doesn't fall in. This may take a few tries to get right. Put a piece of masking tape at the broken end of each toothpick to hold it in place.

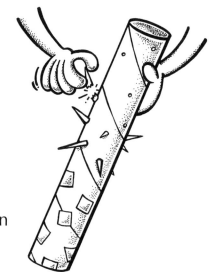

What did the leopard say after eating its owner? *"Man, that hit the spot."*

3 Seal up one end of the tube with electrical tape. Rest the sealed end of the tube on the floor and put the funnel in the top of the tube. Pour the rice, beads, gravel, popcorn, or sand through the funnel and listen to the sound. Try different combinations of things until you get a sound you like, then seal up the top of the tube with the electrical tape.

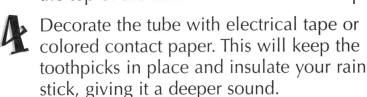

4 Decorate the tube with electrical tape or colored contact paper. This will keep the toothpicks in place and insulate your rain stick, giving it a deeper sound.

HOW YOU CAN HELP SAVE THE RAIN FORESTS

1. Choose cereals, cookies, and nuts that are made from rain-forest products and that advertise the companies' support for rain-forest preservation.
2. Try to buy tree-free or recycled paper. One big reason forests are cut is for paper.
3. Find out which companies are being boycotted for their active participation in the destruction of rain forests and start a student petition that asks your school to avoid using products from those companies.
4. Organize a fund-raising event to raise awareness of the plight of rain forests.
5. Learn as much as you can about rain forests by reading books and surfing the Internet, then tell others about what you've learned. Education is the best tool for action.

Spoon-i-Licious!

Hot chocolate is one of the best antidotes to a rough day at school. The next time you come home after a tough day, dip one of these chocolate-covered spoons into a steaming cup of cocoa and stir. Mmmmm! It's true chocolate perfection! They're great as holiday gifts, too.

What you'll need:

➡ 1 package (12 ounces) milk chocolate chips

⇨ medium-size microwave-safe bowl

➡ mixing spoon

⇨ 2 cookie sheets

➡ wax paper

⇨ 20 heavy plastic spoons

➡ ½ package (6 ounces) white chocolate chips

⇨ chocolate sprinkles or colored sugar crystals

➡ clear gift-wrapping cellophane and ribbon (optional)

What to do:

1 Place the milk chocolate chips into the bowl. Microwave for 1 minute and 30 seconds on high. Take out the bowl and stir the chips, then microwave for another 30 seconds. Take the bowl out and stir again. Continue to microwave for 30-second periods, stirring in between, until all the chips are melted.

2 Line the cookie sheets with wax paper. Dip each spoon into the chocolate, covering the base of the spoon's bowl. Place the dipped spoons on the cookie sheets, and put them in the freezer for about 10 minutes to let them set completely.

What do you call a chicken at the North Pole? **Lost.**

3 Wash the bowl and dry it completely. Once the chocolate on the spoons is set, pour the white chocolate chips into the bowl and melt as in step 1. (White chocolate may take more time to melt than milk chocolate.)

4 Dip each spoon in the white chocolate to cover the bowl of the spoon halfway, creating a layered effect. Return the spoons to the cookie sheets. Let them sit for 5 minutes, or until the chocolate has partially set.

5 Gently scatter the chocolate sprinkles or sugar crystals over the white chocolate-covered tips. Place the spoons in the freezer for another 20 minutes.

6 To store the spoons, keep them in a plastic bag in a cool cupboard away from sunlight. You can also wrap the spoons individually in cellophane and tie the neck of each spoon with ribbon to give them as gifts.

7 Make a cup of hot cocoa or hot milk, then put the spoon in and stir for a Spoon-i-licious treat!

To make the perfect cup of hot cocoa: Fill a microwave-safe mug with milk, then microwave on high for 30 seconds. Take it out and stir, then microwave for another 30 seconds. Pour 1 to 2 heaping tablespoons of cocoa mix into the hot milk, then stir. Top it with whipped cream and dip in one of your chocolate spoons for the perfect sweet treat!

COMET BALL

This is an easy-to-make variation on the tired old game of catch. When tossed in the air, this ball flies like a comet across the sky.

What you'll need:

➡ scissors

⇨ pair of old stockings or tights (make sure you have permission to use them)

➡ tennis ball

What to do:

1 Cut off one leg of the stockings or tights and throw the rest away. Put the ball into the toe of the stocking. (Or cut off both legs and make two Comet Balls!)

2 Tie a knot in the stocking just above the ball.

3 Go outside, hold it by the comet's tail (the open end of the stocking leg), swing it around your head a few times, let go, and watch it fly.

4 If you are playing catch with someone, to catch it, grab the tail as it passes you.

Make up games to play with your Comet Ball. Have contests to see who can throw it the farthest or most accurately, play Monkey in the Middle (also known as Keep-Away), or even organize a modified game of touch football.

The Coolest Crown in Town

This beautiful door ornament also makes a great crown for a costume.

What you'll need:

➡ 10 to 15 silk flowers with wire stems

⇨ grapevine wreath from a craft store

What to do:

1 Weave the flowers and their stems through the grapevine wreath, arranging the flowers so that they are spaced evenly.

2 Once you are happy with the placement of the flowers, bend the wire stems to lock the flowers in place. Poke the ends of the wires into the wreath so there are no sharp edges sticking out.

3 Hang the wreath on your bedroom door or wall, or wear it on your head and feel like royalty for the day.

What do you call a fairy who never takes a bath? *Stinkerbell!*

Bird Sanctuary

Create a feathered-friend vacation home and make a bird family happy!

What you'll need:

➡ newspapers

➡ smock or old shirt

➡ white glue

➡ ½-gallon cardboard milk carton, empty, clean, and dry

➡ ruler

➡ scissors

➡ small dowel stick, ⅛ inch in diameter and 1 inch long

➡ pencil

➡ 4-inch square of heavy cardboard

➡ 4 x 6-inch rectangle of heavy cardboard

➡ acrylic paint, 3 or more colors

➡ paintbrushes

➡ rubber cement

➡ 10-inch piece of twine

➡ birdseed or sunflower seeds

What to do:

1 Spread newspapers over your work space and on the floor. Put on a smock or old shirt to protect your clothes.

2 Glue the pour spout of the milk carton closed. When the glue is dry, cut off ½ inch of the top of the milk carton.

Why did the chicken cross the playground? **To get to the other slide.**

3 Measure 3 inches up from the bottom of the carton in the center of one side, and poke the dowel through to make a hole. Take out the dowel and put it aside.

4 Use a pencil to create guidelines 1 inch above and to the left and right of the hole you just made, and another line 3 inches above the new guideline. Stick the scissors into the hole and cut along those lines to make a rectangular hole 3 inches high and 2 inches wide. This is the door to the birdhouse.

5 Glue the 4-inch square of cardboard to the bottom of the milk carton for a base. Fold the 4 x 6-inch piece of cardboard gently in half, and glue it to the top of the milk carton for a roof.

6 Paint the birdhouse as you'd like. It can feature your favorite sports team's colors, a picture of a popular cartoon character, images of birds, or a rainbow of colors. Paint the dowel as well. Let it dry.

7 Dip the dowel into the rubber cement and poke it through the hole for a perch for the birds. Hold it for a few seconds to let it set. Wipe off any excess rubber cement after it dries.

8 Using the scissors, poke a small hole in each end of the roof. Thread one end of the twine through each hole and tie in a knot on the underside of the roof. This is the hanger.

9 Scatter some birdseed or sunflower seeds on the floor inside your bird sanctuary as an invitation for passing birds. Hang your birdhouse on a branch of a nearby tree and wait to see who moves in! Instead of hanging your birdhouse from a tree, you can also set it on your windowsill or porch.

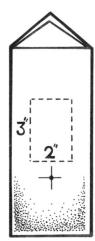

Wrap It Up

Some people say the hardest part of buying a gift is wrapping it. Here's an easy and inexpensive way to wrap a present, whether it's shaped like a basketball or a small book.

What you'll need:

→ newspapers

⇨ smock or old shirt

→ scissors

⇨ kitchen sponges (new, not used)

→ plain paper grocery bag

⇨ tempera paint, at least 2 different colors

→ disposable bowls (1 for each color of paint)

⇨ paper cups filled with water (1 for each color of paint)

→ small shopping bags with handles

⇨ shoe box

→ small plain cards and envelopes (available at florists or craft stores)

What to do:

1 Cover your work space and the floor with newspapers and put on a smock or old shirt. This can get messy!

2 Cut the sponges into different shapes such as stars or clouds. For a challenge, cut a sponge into a circle, then cut out two eyes and a smile from the inside of the sponge to make a happy face.

3 Cut down one side of the plain paper bag along the corner to the bottom. Cut out the bottom so that the bag is now one long sheet. If there is writing on the bag, flip it so that the writing is facedown on the table.

4 Pour paint into the disposable bowls. Dip a sponge into one of the bowls of paint and let the extra paint drip off the sponge. Place the sponge firmly onto the paper, then lift it up and look at the mark. If it looks smudged, you may have moved the sponge too much while pressing down on the paper. If it looks gooey, then you have too much paint on the sponge. If it's too light, you'll need to use more paint.

5 Keep experimenting, using all the sponge shapes. Before using the same sponge with a different color paint, wash out the sponge in one of the paper cups of water and wring it out well. This brown bag is not just a practice page—it can also be homemade wrapping paper. When the sheet is covered and you like the results, set it aside to dry.

6 Now you are ready to decorate your shopping bags. Place a shoe box inside the shopping bag to keep the shape of the bag while you work. Sponge-paint each bag, making sure to cover all sides.

7 If you want a matching card and envelope, sponge-paint the front of each plain card and envelope, then set them aside to dry.

8 Let the finished paper, bags, and cards dry completely before using them as wrapping.

To wrap a present in a gift bag, line the bag with a few pieces of tissue paper or thin colored paper before putting the present in. Tie the handles closed with a curly ribbon or some colored string. You can also sandwich the handles between two stickers.

Cinnamon Photo Gallery

Why does this set of rustic picture frames look and smell like cinnamon? Because they're made out of cinnamon sticks!

What you'll need:

➡ craft glue

➡ ruler

➡ 4 cinnamon sticks

➡ five 4-inch pieces of twine or raffia

➡ pencil

➡ cardboard

➡ scissors

➡ parchment or craft paper

➡ photo

➡ paper towel

What to do:

1. Place a large dot of craft glue ¼ inch from the edge of a cinnamon stick. Hold it against another cinnamon stick at a right angle ¼ inch from its edge. Tie the two sticks together by winding a piece of twine or raffia over and around the corners of each stick. Hold the twine in place with a dot of glue on the back of the frame. Let the ends of the twine stick out to make it look more rustic.

2. Repeat step 1 with the other two sticks, then fasten them all together using the glue and one piece of twine for each corner.

3 Trace your cinnamon square onto the cardboard and cut it out. Trace the cardboard onto the parchment or craft paper and cut that out as well. Glue the paper square onto the cardboard.

4 Tie both ends of the remaining piece of twine to one of the cinnamon sticks to form a hanger. This is now the top of your frame.

5 Measure your photo against the paper square you just made. Carefully cut the photo to fit that size. Make sure you don't cut out any important parts of the photo. You may need to choose from a few photos to find one that is the right size and shape to fit your frame.

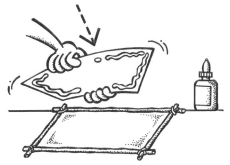

6 Glue along the back of your cinnamon square and place it on the paper side of your cardboard backing. Glue the back of your photo and carefully center it in the frame with the top of the photo at the top of your frame. Using a paper towel, press lightly on the photo to make it stick to the paper backing.

7 Make an entire set for different size photos or to give to friends and family for a great-smelling photo gallery!

What do you call a boomerang that doesn't come back to you? *A stick.*

Face Stickups

There's nothing that cheers you up better than the sight of your best friend's goofy face smiling at you. If you can't be there all the time for your friend, though, don't worry—give your pal your goofiest pic to stick up in a locker and your friend will never feel alone.

What you'll need:

➡ juice bottle lid (Snapple® lids work well)

⇨ pencil

➡ small photo of you (the goofier the better)

⇨ scissors

➡ strong glue

⇨ magnet

What to do:

1. Wash the juice bottle lid well and dry it. Trace the juice lid on the back of the photo, making sure the picture fits in the center.

2. Cut the photo along the line you just traced, and place the photo inside the lid. It should snap inside the lip of the lid and stay put. If it doesn't, dab a little glue on the back of the photo, then place it inside the lid.

3 Glue the magnet on the back of the lid and let it dry for at least 20 minutes.

4 Give it to a friend!

HOW TO CHEER UP A FRIEND

1. Decorate his or her locker with wrapping paper, notes, or balloons.
2. Send your friend a thank-you card for always making you feel good when you're feeling down.
3. Plan a surprise un-birthday party in homeroom before class starts.
4. Bake a big batch of cookies and leave them on your friend's desk in class.
5. Make a list of all the things you like best about your pal and leave it where he or she will find it.

NICOLE'S LOCKER

SAVE YOUR PLACE

Are you hooked on books but always seem to lose your place? Don't dog-ear those pages. Make a bundle of bookmarks that are just your style. They make great gifts for friends and family, too!

What you'll need:

➡ ruler

➡ pencil

➡ construction paper or poster board

➡ scissors

➡ hole punch

➡ tassels or ribbon

➡ rubber stamps and ink pad or stickers

➡ markers or colored pencils

➡ clear, self-adhesive paper

➡ glitter (optional)

What to do:

1 Measure out as many 2 x 6-inch rectangles as you can fit on the construction paper or poster board. You'll have bookmarks for every occasion—schoolbooks, comic books, and even the TV listings!

2 Cut out the rectangles. Using a hole punch, make a hole near the top of each of the rectangles. Thread a tassel or piece of ribbon through the hole.

3 Decorate your bookmarks with rubber stamps or stickers, and draw your own designs using markers or colored pencils.

4. To make a bookworm bookmark, punch overlapping holes along the bottom right-hand corner of the bookmark so it looks as though the corner has been bitten off. Draw a satisfied-looking bookworm in the middle of the bookmark. Color it and write a fun message such as "I just love books" or simply "Burp!"

5. Cover the bookmarks with clear, self-adhesive paper to make them last longer. To make a sparkly or snowy bookmark, sprinkle glitter on the sticky side of the self-adhesive paper, then attach it to the front or back of your bookmark. Trim off the edges using your scissors.

6. Make as many bookmarks as you'd like, then give them to friends or use them for books all over your house!

Potpourri Pizzazz

Do your sneakers stink up your closet? Does your room need a little freshening up? Create a potpourri of potpourri and breathe easy! Below are three recipes for very different kinds of scents. The first is spicy, the second is flowery, and the third smells more woodsy. Create the mixture that sounds best to you, then make the potpourri jars described on page 45 for a great home scent or a nice-smelling present.

Spice Up Your Life
What you'll need:

➡ ¼ cup ground dried cloves

⇨ 4 cinnamon sticks, broken into pieces about ¼ inch each

➡ ½ cup ground allspice

⇨ dried orange peel from one orange, cut into strips

➡ medium-size bowl

⇨ lavender or rose oil

➡ plastic toothpick (if the oil doesn't come with its own dropper)

⇨ plastic wrap

What to do:

1 To make dry orange peel, peel the orange and chop the peel into small pieces. Place the peel in a paper bag and clip it together tightly with a paper clip, and leave it there for 2 weeks or until completely dried out. Or, you can buy dried orange peel from a health food or craft store.

2 Mix all of the ingredients together in a bowl except for the flower oil.

3 Using the dropper or a toothpick, put 20 drops of the flower oil into the bowl.

4 Seal the bowl with plastic wrap, then shake the bowl so that all the ingredients are mixed well.

Romance
What you'll need:

➡ 2 cups dried rose petals in a variety of colors

⇨ medium-size bowl

➡ 2 to 4 stalks of baby's breath flowers

⇨ rose oil

➡ clean plastic toothpick (if the rose oil doesn't come with its own dropper)

⇨ plastic wrap

What to do:

1 Place the dried rose petals in the bowl.

2 Shake the flower buds from the baby's breath into the bowl.

3 Put 20 drops of rose oil into the mixture using the dropper or by dipping the plastic toothpick into the oil and letting it drip into the bowl.

4 Seal the bowl with plastic wrap, then shake the bowl well to combine all the ingredients together. If you use your hands to mix it, beware that the scent will be difficult to wash off!

A Walk in the Woods
What you'll need:

➡ 1 cup different kinds of evergreen needles, dried and washed (you can collect dried needles from the ground near evergreen trees)

⇨ ½ cup miniature pinecones

➡ 2 teaspoons orrisroot powder (from a craft or health food store)

⇨ pine-scented fixative (from a craft store)

➡ clean plastic toothpick (if fixative doesn't come with its own dropper)

⇨ medium-size bowl

➡ plastic wrap

What to do:

1 Mix the pine needles and pinecones in the bowl.

2 Add the orrisroot and 2 drops of the fixative with a toothpick or the dropper that comes with the oil.

3 Seal the bowl with plastic wrap, then shake the bowl well to combine all the ingredients.

Potpourri Jars
What you'll need:

➡️ potpourri

➡️ 4 baby food jars (no lids)

➡️ 6-inch square of thin cotton fabric

➡️ scissors

➡️ 4 ribbons

What to do:

1 Divide your potpourri into the four baby food jars. Cut the cotton fabric into four 3-inch squares. Place one piece of fabric over the mouth of each jar and tie it with a ribbon.

2 If the potpourri starts to lose its scent, shake it a bit to release more of the yummy aromas. You can also add scented oil or more ingredients to your potpourri to refresh the scent.

To dry flowers, wrap a rubber band around the stems, then tie a string to the stems. Tie the other end of the string to a hanger so that the buds are facing down and the stems are straight up in the air.
Hang them away from direct sunlight for at least 2 weeks.

Best-Friend Charms

These matching charms will remind you of your best friend whenever you are apart.

What you'll need:

→ gold chocolate coin

⇨ ballpoint pen

→ 2 necklace chains

⇨ white glue

→ scissors

What to do:

1 Carefully unwrap your chocolate coin, saving both sides of the foil wrapper. Wash and dry the wrapper carefully. Place the pieces on a flat surface. (Feel free to eat your chocolate any time!)

2 Using the flat end of the pen, rub the pieces of coin wrapper to remove any design. They should be as smooth as possible.

3 If your necklace chains are silver, turn the silver side of the foil to the outside. If your chains are gold, the gold will be the outside of the charm.

4 Write on the front of one of the wrapper pieces with a pen, lightly at first. It won't leave a pen mark but will just carve a groove in the foil. You can write "Best Friends" or anything else that might have meaning for both of you. If you make a mistake, rub it out lightly with the flat end of the pen. When you are satisfied with your design, go over the design a few times in pen, strongly enough so that your message appears in ink, but be careful not to tear a hole in the foil. If you do tear a hole in the foil, eat another piece of chocolate and use the new foil wrapper!

5 Draw a jagged line lightly down the center of the back of the charm using the pen.

6 Dab some glue on the inside of the front of the charm and attach it to the inside of the back of the charm. Squeeze out the excess glue, and crimp the edges together to firmly attach them.

7 Use scissors to cut the charm in two along the jagged line on the back. Poke a small hole into the top center of each charm, not too close to the top and large enough for the chain to fit through.

8 Thread a charm onto each chain. Give one to your best friend, and keep one for yourself!

Porcu-Pincushion

This little porcupine is so friendly, it will give you the quills off its back!

What you'll need:

➡️ newspapers

⇨ smock or old shirt

➡️ black modeling clay

⇨ square piece of cardboard

➡️ plastic spoon

⇨ plastic knife

➡️ 2 small white seed beads

⇨ fiberfill or cotton balls

➡️ 6-inch square piece of black cloth

⇨ scissors

➡️ craft glue

⇨ pins

What to do:

1 Spread newspapers all around your work area and on the floor. Put on the smock or old shirt.

2 Roll the clay into a ball. Set the ball firmly on the cardboard and press down slightly to flatten out the bottom. This will be the body of your porcupine.

3 Using the plastic spoon, scoop out some clay from the top of the ball so it forms a bowl. Roll the clay you've just scooped out of the center into two balls of equal size.

4. Using the plastic knife, cut one ball into four small porcupine legs. Attach each of the four pieces to the sides of the large, scooped-out ball. Take a small piece from the remaining ball and attach it to the back of your porcupine for a tail.

5. Mold the rest of the ball into a head, shaping one side to form a small, pointed nose, and pulling the other side to form a thick neck. Attach the neck to the body of the porcupine. Poke the white seed beads into the head to make the eyes. Make a smile, cheeks, and dimples using the knife.

6. Carefully insert the plastic knife between the porcupine and the cardboard base a little at a time to separate the clay from the cardboard. Reinforce any pieces that have come loose. Set the porcupine gently back on the cardboard and let it harden for about a half hour.

7. Fill the scooped-out center of the porcupine's body with fiberfill or cotton balls. Place the fabric over the porcupine and cut a circle about 1 inch larger in circumference than the scooped-out center. Put the circle of fabric on top of the fiberfill, tucking the edges of the fabric into the clay base. Pull out a small piece of fabric and glue it to the inside top edge of the porcupine's body. Go around the edge, taking and gluing small sections of fabric at a time. Poke pins all over the fabric so they stick up like a porcupine's quills.

8. Set your porcupine to dry in a dark, cool place where it won't get knocked over. It's best not to move it off the cardboard for a few days until it is completely dry.

9. After your porcu-pal is dry, place it wherever you think it will be the handiest. It makes a great friend, but whatever you do, don't pet it!

What do you call a gorilla wearing earmuffs? **Anything you like—he can't hear you.**

Your Very Own Journal

A journal is a place where you keep important information such as personal or creative stories, poems, travel notes, or a log of your daily activities. You can also use it as an assignment book or day planner.

What you'll need:

- 2 to 3 feet of fabric
- hardcover notebook or blank book
- pencil
- ruler
- scissors
- ribbon
- glue
- ink pad and stamp (optional)

What to do:

1. Lay the fabric out on your work space. Open the book and lay it down on the fabric. Using your pencil and ruler, draw a rectangle on the fabric 1 inch larger than the outline of your open book. Cut out the rectangle with the scissors.

2. Hold the ribbon against the book, and cut it to measure at least 2 inches longer than the length of the book. Center the ribbon inside the book near the binding so that an equal amount hangs out from the top and bottom of the book. Glue the top of the ribbon to the outside front cover of the book near the binding. This is your placeholder.

What starts with *t*, ends with *t*, and is full of *t*? **A teapot.**

3 Open the book and center it on the fabric rectangle you cut out. Cut two slits in the fabric along the top and bottom of the book near the binding and fold the flaps into the inside covers.

4 Glue the edges of the fabric to the inside front and back covers, gluing first the top and bottom flaps, then the sides.

5 You can decorate your book further by gluing fabric cutouts to the cover. You can also jazz up the journal's pages by stamping small, colorful designs in the margins.

6 Keep your journal someplace safe, far from prying eyes.

Did you know...

that some of history's most famous people, including soldiers, prisoners, lawyers, detectives, slaves, dancers, actors, and musicians kept journals? Reading their journals and memoirs teaches us a great deal about others and the times they lived in. Some famous journal-writers are:

The Diary of a Young Girl, by **Anne Frank**

Farewell to Manzanar: A True Story of Japanese American Experience During and After the World War Internment, by **Jeanne Wakatsuki Houston**

Red Scarf Girl: A Memoir of the Cultural Revolution, by **Ji-Li Jiang**

Wren, by **Marie Killilea**

Pebbles with Personality

Turn a cold stone into a warm creature in minutes by drawing out the natural personality of a pet rock.

What you'll need:

➡ rock

⇨ paper towels

➡ white glue

⇨ googly eyes

➡ yarn

⇨ other accessories, as needed (paper clips, glitter, seed beads, felt, etc.)

What to do:

1 Set out on a rock hunt. Your mission is to find the perfect rock with just the right personality. Do you want a flat, solid-looking stone? Or perhaps a perky little pebble, just right for a pocket?

2 When you've found your new "pet," wash it with soap and water and put it on a towel to dry.

3 Take a look at your rock. Choose its good side, and place that side facing you on a paper towel. Dab some glue on an eye, and place it on the rock. Hold it for a few seconds until it sets. Wipe away any excess glue with a paper towel or your finger. Keep adding eyes until you're satisfied with the result.

4 Using yarn, glue on the mouth and hair, and wipe away excess glue. Add accessories such as paper-clip glasses, glitter or seed-bead earrings, or a felt bow tie. Give your rock a name, and place it on your desk as a paper-weight, in your locker, or on top of your computer.

How does a girl vampire flirt with a boy vampire? **She bats her eyes at him.**

CRAZY DOUGH

Poke it, pull it, stretch it, and bounce it—this stuff does it all, and you can make it right in your kitchen! This mixture may not work on humid or rainy days.

What you'll need:

➡ 1 cup liquid starch

⇨ 2 cups Elmer's® white glue (other glue has too much water in it and may not work as well)

➡ bowl

⇨ spoon

➡ airtight container with lid

What to do:

1 Mix the starch and glue together in the bowl. If your dough does not seem rubbery enough, add more starch, a tablespoon at a time. Set the mixture aside to dry. Clean up your work area while it's drying.

2 Touch the dough every 5 minutes. When it's solid, push, pull, bounce, and play with it all you want!

3 When you're done playing with your Crazy Dough, store it in the container for next time. It will keep for a few weeks, as long as you keep the container sealed tight.

Warning:
This dough will stain carpets and furniture. Only play with it on top of newspaper and wax paper, or outside.

How do skunks communicate with each other? **They use smell phones.**

Favorite Pal Keepsake Book

Homework, tests, and pop quizzes are some school memories most kids would probably rather forget. But the great times spent with friends working together on projects, hanging out after school, and generally having a good time are memories worth preserving forever. Create a scrapbook and look back with your friends months or years from now and enjoy these days all over again.

What you'll need:

➡ flat souvenirs (such as napkin drawings, notes passed in class, ticket stubs, newspaper ads, baseball cards, box tops, or dried pressed flowers)

➡ photos you can cut up

➡ photo album with sticky pages (not one with slots for photos)

➡ construction paper

➡ colored markers

➡ clear, self-adhesive paper, the same size as the album

What to do:

1 Spread your souvenirs and photos out on your work space and take a look at what you have collected.

2 Arrange things in sections. You can group it chronologically (in the order that things happened), divide everything according to a theme, or use it all to tell a story.

3 Once you have your materials in the order you want, separate everything into pages. Keep in mind whether you'll be using one or both sides of each page of the photo album, and if you want to use single-page or double-page layouts.

What dogs love to have their hair washed? **Sham-poodles!**

4 Reserve a few of your favorite items to decorate the album's cover.

5 Arrange the items for each layout on the floor. You can cut up the photos into fun shapes, cut around people's faces, or leave them as is. You can mount them on construction paper or on a background of souvenirs. Use the construction paper and markers to create labels for each page, labeling the theme of the page, inserting a quote from a famous movie or favorite conversation, or telling a story throughout all the pages.

6 Open the clear film on an album page and carefully transfer your souvenirs and photos to the page. Be sure to leave enough white space so that the adhesive can stick to the page and keep your things from falling out or getting moved around. If you are layering items on the page, you may want to put a dab of glue on the back of the top items so they do not shift around.

7 Do the same for each page until all of the pages have been filled or you run out of souvenirs. It's OK to have empty pages at the end. You can just keep adding to the book as you get more photos and memorabilia.

8 Take the reserved items and arrange them on the cover of your photo album. Put a dab of glue on the back of each one, and glue them on the cover.

9 Begin to peel off one edge of the backing on the self-adhesive paper, and line it up with the edge of the book. Hold the backing with one hand and peel it off slowly while smoothing the paper onto the cover with the other hand, preventing it from buckling. Keep this wonderful memory book on your bookshelf, or wrap the book and give it as a present.

Lighter-than-Air Glider

Make a plane out of recycled Styrofoam® that flies and floats!

What you'll need:

➡ pen
⇨ ruler
➡ 3 clean Styrofoam® trays
⇨ scissors
➡ plastic knife
⇨ waterproof markers
➡ paper clip

What to do:

1 Draw a 2 x 8-inch rectangle on one Styrofoam® tray. Cut it out and round the edges slightly with your scissors, then set it aside. This forms the wings.

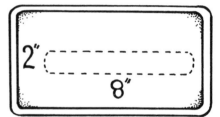

2 On the second tray, draw another 2 x 8-inch rectangle. This is the base for the body of the plane. With scissors, round one end of the body for the nose of the plane, and create a small dome 1½ inches back from the nose for the cockpit. Add a tail to the back end of the body that comes out at a slight angle and measures 1½ inches up from the top of the rectangle and 1 inch in toward the body. (See the illustration.) Cut it out.

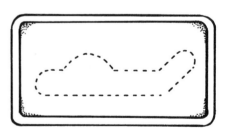

3 On a Styrofoam® scrap or on the remaining tray, cut out one last 1½ x 4-inch rectangle. Round the edges slightly using your scissors. This is the plane's tail cross-piece.

4. To connect the pieces, first lay the Styrofoam® body on the table and, using your ruler, mark 3 inches and 5 inches from the back of the plane and 1 inch up from the bottom. Draw a line to mark it off. Carefully cut along the line using the plastic knife to make a slit in the body of the plane.

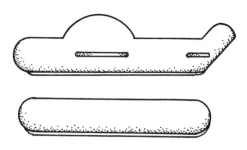

5. Draw a line that begins 1 inch up from the bottom and ½ inch from the back of the plane and continues toward the front of the plane for 1 inch. Cut along the line carefully with the plastic knife.

6. Using your markers, design your plane with colors or details. Insert the small rectangle from step 3 carefully into the slit at the back of the plane. Insert the large rectangle from step 1 carefully into the slit at the middle of the plane. Place the paper clip on the nose of the plane, pointing back toward the tail. This will help your plane fly better.

7. You now have a plane that can float and fly! Test it out in the sink or take it for a test fly outside. It can even land on water!

HANG IT UP

Are you always losing things like your keys or jewelry? Hang it up on this handy hook-board that's easy to make and fun to decorate.

What you'll need:

➡ newspapers

⇨ smock or old shirt

➡ 10 x 2 x 1-inch piece of balsa wood or other soft wood (can be longer or shorter)

⇨ work gloves or gardening gloves

➡ sandpaper

⇨ ruler

➡ pencil

⇨ 4 small cup hooks with screw ends (from a hardware store)

➡ tempera paint

⇨ paintbrushes

➡ 2 self-adhesive hanging brackets

What to do:

1 Cover your work space with newspapers and put on your smock or old shirt.

2 If your wood looks like it may have a few splinters, put on your gloves and lightly sand all the edges until they're smooth.

3 Using your ruler and pencil, draw a straight line along the center of the longest part of the board by measuring 1 inch down from the top. Along that line, mark off 1 inch from one end of the board.

4. Make another mark 2 inches from the 1-inch mark. Measure another 2 inches and make another mark. Do this two more times so that you have four marks along the center line, each spaced 2 inches apart, with the marks on the end sitting 1 inch from each end.

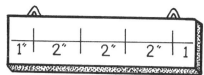

5. Gently twist the screw end of the first cup hook into the first mark you made. It should go in fairly easily. Make sure you are turning the right way. Don't screw it in all the way. Twist the remaining three cup hooks into the other marks, though not too tightly. Take out all four hooks so that you can paint the block.

6. Paint the block of wood with a design, your name, or the name of your favorite rock group or sports team. Set it aside to dry.

7. Screw the four cup hooks back into their holes in the wood, this time screwing them all the way into the wood.

8. Attach the self-adhesive hanging brackets to the back of your board, even with the first and last hooks on the front. Have a parent or grown-up hang it up for you.

9. Hang your keys, necklaces, or other light objects on your board.

Dream Catcher

According to a Native American legend, dreams are messages from the spirit world. If you hang a dream catcher over your bed, it will trap the bad dreams in the web until the next day, when they disappear in the morning sunlight. The good dreams will pass through the center of the web and go back to you.

What you'll need:

➡ 2 pipe cleaners or 12 inches of bendable wire

➡ clothespin

➡ 4 yards (12 feet) of ribbon

➡ ruler

➡ glue

➡ scissors

➡ 3 yards (9 feet) of white cotton string rolled into a ball (bakery string works well)

➡ 24 to 26 beads

➡ feathers (optional)

What to do:

1 Make a ring by twisting the ends of the pipe cleaners or wire together tightly in a circle.

2 Dab some glue on the first inch of the ribbon, then place it on the spot where you twisted the wire ends together.

Why did Silly Billy take a ruler to bed? *He wanted to see how long he slept!*

3 Start wrapping the ribbon around the wire ring, making sure you are covering the wire completely. When you have wrapped about 1 inch of the ribbon, put a clothespin on the end of the ribbon to make it stay put.

4 Continue wrapping the ribbon around the wire, making sure the ribbon lies flat and doesn't twist. When you get back to where you started, cut the ribbon, leaving a little extra for the ribbon to overlap itself at the beginning. Glue the end of the ribbon to the ring and move the clothespin so it holds the end down. Allow the glue to dry.

5 Now it is time to tie the first row of the web. Take the ball of string and tie the end of it around the ring. Dab some glue on the knot so it won't move. Thread the ball of string once around the ring, making a loop. Bring the ball of string through the loop, leaving some slack and not tightening the loop completely. Do this seven more times going around the circle, making seven more loops. Stop when you get back to where you glued the first knot to the ring. Tie a knot and cut the string.

6 To make the next row, take the ball of string and tie the end to the first loop you made in the first row. Bring the string around the circle, making eight loops like you did before. When you get to the end, tie it off with a good solid knot and cut the string. For the third row, do the exact same thing, making eight more loops and tying a knot at the end.

7 To make the hanger, cut the remaining ribbon into four 12-inch pieces. Set three aside.

8 Fold one ribbon in half and knot the two ends together. If you would like, for extra decoration, you can add a few beads to the ribbon before you tie it. Attach the hanger to the top of the ring by slipping the loop end through the ring, around the ring, and then through the ribbon so it forms a knot. Pull tight.

9 Knot one end of each of the three remaining ribbons. Thread two to four beads onto each ribbon, then tie a knot in the other end. The knots must be big enough so that the beads do not fall off the ribbon.

10 Slide one or two beads on one end of each ribbon and one or two beads on the other. Fold each ribbon in half. Tie the first ribbon to the bottom of the ring (the opposite side of the hanger) so that the two ends with two beads each dangle down from the Dream Catcher. Tie the second and third ribbons on either side of the first ribbon. If you would like, you can glue feathers to each of the dangling ribbons.

11 Hang the Dream Catcher in your room above your bed. May your dreams be sweet, and may your nightmares get tangled in the web of the Dream Catcher.

ID Tags

Create a set of army-style dog tags to wear around your neck or to clip to your backpack or gym bag.

What you'll need:

→ ruler
⇨ scissors
→ small piece of thick cardboard
⇨ aluminum foil
→ hole punch
⇨ paper towel
→ pen
⇨ ball chain, 18 inches for a neck chain, 6 inches for a key chain (available at a hardware store)

What to do:

1 Measure and cut out two 1½ x 2¼-inch rectangles from the cardboard for the tags. Trim each corner of the tags to round the edges. Cover the tags with aluminum foil. With the hole punch, make a hole in each tag ¼ inch from the top.

2 For cushion, place the tags on a folded paper towel, and draw or write on the front of each tag by pressing lightly on it with your pen. If you go over your design a few times lightly, it produces better results than carving it once pressing very hard. You can write your name in fancy script. Or, maybe there is an object that you think represents you, such as a rainbow, sports car, dolphin, or unicorn. Draw it! Finally, string the tags, back sides together, onto the ball chain.

MAKE A PEOPLE FEEDER

Birds use bird feeders. Why can't we have people feeders? You don't know? Well, then, let's fix this situation right away! Here is an easy craft you can make out of a used milk carton and some paint.

What you'll need:

➡ 1-quart cardboard milk carton, empty, clean, and dry

⇨ pen

➡ ruler

⇨ scissors

➡ glue

⇨ paper or plastic plate

➡ construction paper

⇨ old magazines (make sure everyone in the house is finished reading them first!)

➡ markers or acrylic paint and paintbrush (optional)

⇨ paper clip

➡ people food, such as candy or nuts (make sure the food is dry and does not need to be refrigerated)

What to do:

1 Draw a little door flap about 1½ inches wide and 1½ inches high on the bottom of the milk carton. Cut the bottom and sides of the flap so that the door is attached at the top and swings up to open. To make the first cut, carefully poke a hole along the bottom line using your pen, then cut the rest using your scissors.

2 Glue the bottom of the carton to the plate to create a stand and to catch any flyaway food. Using glue, cover the entire carton with construction paper so none of the carton is showing. Keep the spout unglued so you can pour the people food in when you're done.

3 While the glue dries, look through the magazines and cut out pictures of things you like, such as faces, houses, trees, or words. You can try to make a theme or put a scene together. Glue the pictures to the milk carton. If you don't want to use magazine pictures, you can decorate the construction paper with markers or paint.

4 Poke the end of the paper clip near the bottom of the right side of the door and slide it toward the side of the carton to form a door latch. To open the door, twist the paper clip up. To lock it, twist the clip to the side.

5 Fill 'er up! Open the spout of the carton and fill the carton with your favorite snack, such as raisins, nuts, or trail mix. Make sure the food will fit through the door flap in the bottom! Share and enjoy!

Stained-Glass Sun Catchers

Sunlight shining through a window can make some interesting patterns on the floor. With this Stained-Glass Sun Catcher, sunshine can be turned into a work of art.

What you'll need:

➡ scissors

⇨ 2 sheets of clear acrylic plastic

➡ ruler

⇨ plain piece of paper

➡ pencil

⇨ 2 pieces of colored tissue paper (1 light color, 1 dark color)

➡ glue

⇨ paper plate

➡ paintbrush

⇨ glitter

➡ hole punch

⇨ string or ribbon

What to do:

1 Cut the sheets of clear plastic into two 4-inch squares.

2 Draw a 4-inch square on the plain paper with your pencil. Draw a simple design inside the square such as a heart, a hand-print, a fish, or an outline of your favorite

animal. It should not touch any of the square's edges. Darken the lines of your design and square so you will be able to see them through the tissue paper.

3 Place the light-colored tissue paper over the paper and trace the square and the design inside it. Cut the square out, then cut the design out of the tissue paper so the hole is in the shape of the design. It's OK if you cut the outside edge of the square by accident. It can be fixed in step 6 when you glue the two sheets together. Keep the outside square and place it to the side. This will be the outline.

4 Place the dark-colored tissue paper over the plain paper and trace and cut out the design. Place the dark cutout inside the lighter-colored square with the hole in it. They should fit together. It's OK if it overlaps in some places or if there are open spaces.

5 Pour a little glue on the paper plate. Use the paintbrush to spread a very thin layer of glue on one of the plastic squares. Carefully place the square of light tissue paper with the hole in it on the plastic sheet. Try not to fold or crumple the tissue paper. Place the darker tissue-paper cutout on the plastic sheet, fitting it into the hole in the other tissue paper.

6 Brush a thin layer of glue on the other plastic square. Sprinkle a tiny bit of glitter onto the glue. Line up the edges of the two plastic sheets and fit them together to make a tissue-paper sandwich. Use the hole punch to make a hole in the top center of the plastic sandwich.

7 Thread the string or ribbon through the hole and tie it at the top. Hang your sun catcher in a window and wait for a sunny day!

Knock, Knock. **Who's there?** Wayne. **Wayne who?** Wayne, Wayne, go away. Come again another day.

LIVELY LAMP SHADES

Light up your life with a personal touch.

What you'll need:

➡ pencil

⇨ plain white drawing paper

➡ small bedroom lamp with a plain white or light-colored lamp shade (available at most discount stores)

⇨ colored pencils

➡ 2-inch piece of string

⇨ hole punch

➡ scissors

⇨ lightweight fishing line

➡ ruler

⇨ prisms and colorful glass beads with holes

What to do:

1 Draw your design on paper. You can make a small design that repeats itself around the shade, or create one whole scene.

2 Turn off and unplug your lamp, then remove the lamp shade. Copy your design lightly onto the lamp shade. Color in your design with colored pencils.

3 Using the 2-inch string, mark off 2-inch intervals along the bottom of the lamp shade.

4 Punch holes along the bottom of the lamp shade at each mark.

5 Count the number of holes you made. Cut the fishing line into as many 6-inch pieces as you have holes. Thread one prism onto each line and fold it in half, with the prism dangling at the bottom.

6 Slip the beads over both ends of the lines to create a pattern on top of the prism.

7 Tie one strand of beads to each hole, and bring the knot inside the lamp shade so it doesn't show.

8 Put the lamp shade on the lamp, plug it in, and turn it on. Check out the cool shadows and patterns your new lamp shade casts around the room!

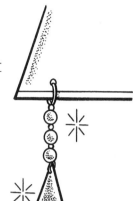

What makes a prism cast rainbows on the wall?
Plain, everyday white light is made out of all the colors of the rainbow coming together. A prism is a many-sided piece of clear glass. When light hits the glass, it's refracted (bent) at different angles, separating the white light into its many colors and creating little rainbows!

Quick Sticks

Stickers can be fun to stick on lockers, book covers, letters, and other places. Wouldn't it be great if you could create your own? You can! Just follow the directions below and you'll be personalizing messages all over town.

What you'll need:

➡ scissors

⇨ magazine pictures, wrapping paper, comic cutouts, or other pictures

➡ measuring spoons

⇨ packet (8-serving size) of flavored gelatin

➡ bowl

⇨ microwave-safe mug filled with water

➡ potholders

⇨ clean paintbrush or pastry brush

➡ resealable plastic bag

⇨ plate or cookie sheet

What to do:

1 Cut out the pictures you want to make into stickers and set them aside. Measure 1 tablespoon gelatin and pour it into the bowl.

2 Microwave the mug of water on high for 1 minute. Remove it from the microwave with potholders—it will be HOT!

3 Measure 2 tablespoons hot water and pour it into the bowl with the gelatin. Stir until the gelatin is dissolved.

4 Let mixture cool for 1 minute, then brush a thin coat on the back of each cutout. If you need more solution, reheat the water and make another batch of the mixture. Put leftover gelatin powder in a resealable plastic bag and label it so that you can use it again next time.

5 Set the cutouts facedown on a plate or cookie sheet to dry. When your stickers are dry, you can lick them and stick them on your locker, books, papers, letters, or bedroom door! (Only stick them on places or things that are yours or where you have permission to decorate.)

You can turn your own designs into stickers as well. Just draw or paint designs on slick blank paper, cut them out, then paint the gelatin solution onto the backs following the directions above.

No-Bake Candy House

Hansel and Gretel's house has inspired many hungry school kids to make their own edible houses. Let your sweet tooth be your inspiration to create this masterpiece that's an after-school activity and snack all in one!

What you'll need:

- cardboard box with top flaps
- cookie sheet
- masking tape
- scissors
- 2 empty paper-towel rolls
- 2 tubes of frosting (don't use tubes of cake frosting—that won't harden)
- rubber spatula
- box of graham crackers
- 2 sugar cones
- a variety of decorative foods, such as little cookies, pretzel sticks, licorice, marshmallows, gumdrops, hard candies, candy canes, non-pareils, gummy bears, and animal crackers

What to do:

1 Place the cardboard box on the cookie sheet with the flaps out. Lean the two flaps on the long side of the box in toward each other, and tape them together with one long strip of masking tape where they come to a point at the top.

2 Hold the two shorter flaps up against the pointed top. Cut the corners off of each of the two flaps, then tape the edges to the sides of the open triangles to complete the roof.

3 Tape one paper-towel roll to each side of the box house you just created to make castle turrets. Spread the frosting all over the house and turrets using your rubber spatula.

4 Spread frosting on the back of a graham cracker and place it on the roof of the house. Hold it there for at least 10 seconds to make sure it sticks. Cover the roof with graham crackers. Put a sugar cone on top of each paper-towel roll turret.

5 Using your decorative foods, add a door, windows, trimmings, a garden, and a path leading up to the door. Spread frosting on each food item and stick it on the graham-cracker house. Hold it for 10 seconds before letting go to make sure it sticks. Since it looks so delicious, it probably won't last very long. So take a photo, then share and enjoy!

Don't get too much of the same kind of candy. It's important to have a selection of different kinds of candies. Buying a Halloween variety pack (always on sale after Halloween and before Christmas!) or making a trip to a pick-a-mix store for a pound or less of candy are the best ways to get a big selection without spending too much money.

CARTOONS TO FLIP OVER

You can make your own animated cartoon very easily, even if you're not the greatest artist in the world.

What you'll need:

➡ 1 medium- or large-size Post-it™ or other brand of sticky-note pad

⇨ pencil

➡ colored pens, pencils, or markers

What to do:

1 Plan your animation in your head. Think of something that you can draw well, such as a running stick-figure, a person smiling and frowning, or a ball bouncing. Make your first animated flip-book very simple so you can get the hang of it.

2 Set the sticky side along the top of the pad. Write a title on the first page. Draw your starting frame in pencil on the second page in the lower right-hand corner. Keep your design toward the edge of the paper, away from the sticky side. Keep the pages attached to the pad.

3 On the third page, draw the figure again, the same size and in the same position as the first frame. Instead of drawing it exactly the same, however, move it slightly in the direction it needs to go. If it's a person running, move his or her arm and leg just slightly as if about to take a step.

4. On the next page, draw the figure once more in the same place and size as the frame before, moving it slightly from the second frame.

5. As you draw each frame, keep flipping back and forth between the frames to see how your figure is progressing.

6. When you have completed the animation, hold the book with your right hand. Using your thumb, flip through all the pages quickly to watch your animation.

7. As you flip back and forth between the frames, you can erase any mistakes or take out a ruined page and insert another blank page in its place from the back of the pad.

8. Once you are satisfied with how your book looks, color the figures on each page to make them come alive even more. You can flesh out your stick figure, decorate the ball, or bring some life into the smiling and frowning face.

9. Flip through it again. Does it work? It does? Great! You've just created your first animated cartoon!

Vegetable Puppets

Put them together, put on a show, and then eat the stars!

What you'll need:

➡ some of your favorite raw vegetables, such as celery, carrots, broccoli, black olives, green olives (with pimentos), mushrooms, green and red peppers

⇨ butter knife

➡ toothpicks

⇨ cream cheese or peanut butter

What to do:

1 Wash the vegetables carefully with water (no soap!) and dry them. Ask a grown-up for help cutting the vegetables, if you need it.

2 Use a large vegetable, such as a carrot, a head of broccoli, a celery stalk, or even a tomato, as the base for your puppet.

3 Pick out pieces of food that would make good eyes, noses, mouths, ears, hats, bow ties—you name it.

4 For larger, heavier face parts, attach them to the base using toothpicks. For smaller, lighter face parts, attach them by spreading a little bit of cream cheese or peanut butter on the base, and sticking the face part to the cream cheese or peanut butter.

5 When you're done with your puppets (don't forget to name them), put on a show at the table.

6 All that work will probably make you very hungry, but that's no problem. Just eat the stars of the show!

What's black-and-white and black-and-white and black-and-white? **A penguin rolling down a hill.**

Chewable Art

With this cool craft, you can have your play clay and eat it, too.

What you'll need:

- 2 cups creamy peanut butter
- 6 tablespoons honey
- mixing bowl
- large spoon
- 2 to 3 cups nonfat dry (powdered) milk
- ⅓ cup cocoa powder for flavor (optional—Hershey's® or Nestlé Nesquik® work well)
- wax paper
- candy decorations (chocolate-covered raisins, gummy bears, raisins, nonpareils, or other favorites)

What to do:

1. Mix together the peanut butter and honey in the bowl. Shake in the dry milk a little at a time and stir. Keep adding dry milk a few shakes at a time until the mixture feels like dough.

2. Add some cocoa powder for flavor if you'd like. Grab a hunk of your dough and place it on the wax paper.

3. Mold it, shape it, and decorate it with the candies. Show your colorful creations to friends and family, then eat them!

4. Place the leftover dough in the refrigerator, wrapped in the wax paper and sealed in a plastic bag. It will last for a couple of days.

Remember, always wash your hands well before playing with your food!

Edible Log Cabin

Build a house just like the one Abraham Lincoln grew up in. Well, sort of—he couldn't eat his house!

What you'll need:

➡ cardboard box with top flaps

➡ cookie sheet

➡ masking tape

➡ scissors

➡ butter knife (or any knife that does not have a sharp edge)

➡ pretzel rods

➡ creamy peanut butter

➡ raisins or flat, square crackers

What to do:

1 Place the cardboard box on the cookie sheet with the flaps out. Lean the two flaps on the long side of the box in toward each other, and tape them together with one long strip of masking tape where they come to a point at the top.

2 Hold the two shorter flaps up against the pointed top. Cut the corners off of each of the two flaps, then tape the edges to the sides of the open triangles to complete the roof.

3 Use the butter knife to spread peanut butter all over the outside of the house.

4. Attach the pretzel rods to the sides of the house, holding each one in place for a few seconds to make sure it sticks. It may take a couple of tries to make some of the pretzels stick.

5. Create a door and windows by spreading peanut butter over some of the pretzels and pressing raisins or crackers onto the peanut butter.

6. Show off your terrific log cabin to your friends, then have them help you eat it!

What do you get when you cross peanut butter with an elephant?
You either get peanut butter that never forgets, or an elephant that sticks to the roof of your mouth.

79

BACK-TO-NATURE BOOKENDS

Collecting things on a nature walk is a lot of fun. Preserve your natural treasures in these useful and decorative bookends.

What you'll need:

➡ newspapers

➡ smock or old shirt

➡ package of modeling clay (about 4 fistfuls)

➡ small objects from nature, such as seashells, beads, or tiny pinecones

➡ small photos (optional)

What to do:

1 Spread newspapers over your work space and on the floor. Put on your smock or old shirt.

2 Split the clay in half. Roll each half into a ball, then pound each ball on the table to flatten it on the bottom. This forms the base.

3 Pick up the clay, turn it a quarter turn, then pound it on the table again to make a corner. Do the same to the other ball, then smooth the rounded part of each ball.

4 Decorate the clay by pressing your objects into the rounded sides of the clay. Reshape the clay and rearrange the objects as you wish. You can also press a small photo into the front of each of your bookends, if you'd like.

5 Let the bookends dry for the amount of time recommended on the clay package. This can take anywhere from a few hours to a few days. When your bookends are dry, set them up on your bookshelf!

 Did you know that someone did a book review of the phone book? *They said it has a great cast of characters but no plot.*